THE ROAD TO Regulation

A story about understanding **FEELINGS** and **EMOTIONS**

Leah Kuypers and Elizabeth Sautter

Illustrated by Fátima Anaya

Think Social Publishing, Inc., Santa Clara, California

www.socialthinking.com

The Zones of Regulation™
The Road to Regulation: A Story About Understanding Feelings and Emotions

Written by Leah M. Kuypers, MA Ed. OTR/L and Elizabeth Sautter, MA, CCC-SLP
www.zonesofregulation.com
The Zones of Regulation™ is a trademark belonging to Leah Kuypers.
Copyright © 2021 Think Social Publishing, Inc.
All Rights Reserved except as noted herein.

Outside of the specific use described below, all other reproduction/copying, adaptation, conversion to electronic format, or sharing/distribution of content, through print or electronic means, is not permitted without written permission from Think Social Publishing, Inc. (TSP).

This includes prohibition of any use of any content or materials from this product as part of an adaptation or derivative work you create for posting on a personal or business website, TeachersPayTeachers, YouTube, Pinterest, Facebook, or any other social media or information sharing site in existence now or in the future, whether free or for a fee. Exceptions are made, upon written request, for product reviews, articles, and blogposts.

Think Social Publishing, Inc. (TSP) grants permission to the owner of this book to use and/or adapt content in print or electronic form, **only** for direct in-classroom/school/home or in-clinic use with your own students/clients/children, and with the primary stakeholders in that individual's life, which includes parents/caregivers and direct service personnel. The copyright for any adaptation of content owned by TSP remains with TSP as a derivative work.

Social Thinking, Superflex, The Unthinkables, The Thinkables, and We Thinkers! GPS are trademarks belonging to TSP. The Zones of Regulation is a trademark belonging to Leah Kuypers, a TSP author.

Translation of this product can only be done in accordance with our TRANSLATION POLICY found on our intellectual property website page here: https://www.socialthinking.com/intellectual-property.

And, visit our intellectual property page to find detailed TERMS OF USE information and a DECISION-TREE that cover copyright, trademark, and intellectual property topics and questions governing the use of our materials.

ISBN: 978-1-936943-60-9 (print)
ISBN: 978-1-936943-70-8 (Zones of Regulation 2-Storybook Set ebook)

Think Social Publishing, Inc.
404 Saratoga Avenue, Suite 200
Santa Clara, CA 95050
Tel: (408) 557-8595
Fax: (408) 557-8594

Illustrated by Fátima Anaya
Book design by Megan Jones Design

This book was printed and bound in the United States by Mighty Color Printing.
TSP is a sole source provider of Social Thinking Products in the U.S.
Books may be purchased online at www.socialthinking.com

Dedicated to all the co-regulators out there who are making a difference in the lives of so many children. Keep up the great work.

Thank you to Gabriel, Julian, Daniel, Vivian, and let's not forget Emma for helping us by providing real-life experiences and your advice on how to share this information.

INTRODUCTION AND RECOMMENDED TEACHING

All day, every day, our body (including our brain) feels sensations, states of alertness (energy), and emotions. They come and go and are influenced by what is happening around us, what we are thinking about, and how we feel. They are not bad or good but can feel comfortable (happy, excited, or warm) or uncomfortable (sad, scared, or over-heated). We use the word "feelings" to describe sensations, emotions, and our states of alertness throughout this storybook. It is okay if children are not familiar with the term *regulation* before beginning this book, it will be explored over this book and the next.

Feelings come in different sizes, intensities, and levels of energy. To make this easy to talk and think about, we can categorize them into four simple, colored categories that we call The Zones of Regulation.

- The **BLUE ZONE** is used to describe low states of alertness and down feelings, such as when a person feels sad, tired, sick, or bored.

- The **GREEN ZONE** is used to describe a calm state of alertness. A person may be described as happy, focused, content, or ready to learn when in the Green Zone. This is the zone where optimal learning occurs.

- The **YELLOW ZONE** is used to describe when our energy is higher and emotions get a little bigger, making it a bit harder to regulate. A person may be experiencing stress, frustration, anxiety, excitement, silliness, the wiggles, or nervousness when in the Yellow Zone.

- The **RED ZONE** is used to describe extremely high energy and intense feelings. A person may be feeling elated, anger, rage, devastation, out of control, or terrified when in the Red Zone.

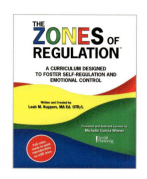

The Zones of Regulation® Curriculum

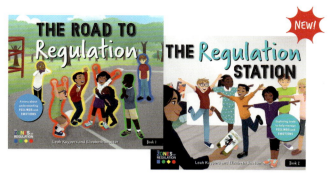

The Road to Regulation (Book 1) and *The Regulation Station* (Book 2)

Tools to Try Cards for Kids

These two children's books were created to provide an easy, kid-friendly way to introduce and support The Zones of Regulation framework, for children developmental ages 5 to 11. They are meant to be used in conjunction with lessons from the curriculum book, *The Zones of Regulation* (Kuypers, 2011). They are a supplement to, not a replacement for, the in-depth lessons found in *The Zones of Regulation* curriculum book. The *Tools to Try Cards for Kids* deck is designed to be used in conjunction with the storybooks and curriculum. *The Road to Regulation* is the first of two stories that starts the conversation and introduces the first steps within the Zones framework. This book can be used in multiple ways: read to a whole classroom of students, used as a therapy tool, read as a bedtime story, or for children to pick up and read on their own. When reading this storybook, take the time to discuss the situations and help children reflect on and process times when they have been in similar situations and how they might have felt. See the Extend the Learning section on page 60 for guided questions and curriculum references, followed by a vocabulary list, activity sheets, and "dos and don'ts" to assist with teaching.

Enjoy,

LEAH and **ELIZABETH**

If one thing is for certain, Gabriel does NOT want to get up. He knows he has to get ready for school but that feels impossible. His body feels heavy and he can barely open his eyes.

Gabriel grabs the rest of his breakfast and backpack and runs outside to meet Suhana and Julian, his neighbors.

"Hi Gabriel," Suhana says with a big smile. "Are you excited about the kickball game today?" she asks enthusiastically.

Before he can answer, Julian sees the bus coming and feels a sense of panic as his heart starts to race. He worries that they might miss the bus. They all sprint down the block to catch it.

As the kids find seats on the bus, they can't help but feel the sensation of their hearts beating so fast . . . thump, thump, thump. Gabriel can barely catch his breath and remembers what his dad mentioned. He notices his body is hot. He pulls off his sweatshirt and takes a deep breath, which helps him cool down. As Julian catches his breath, he notices his muscles relax and the tightness in his chest go away.

"Good morning kids," says Ms. Lee. "We have a busy day planned."

Ms. Lee reviews the schedule, reminding them of the assembly that morning and then asks students to pull out their silent reading books. Gabriel grabs his book. He loves to read and it makes him feel calm and happy.

Vivian hears her name and knows she is expected to say something, but the words don't want to come out. She feels her face, ears, and neck heat up and notices a lump in her throat. "Um, um, um, well, I liked, um, well."

Suddenly, an announcement comes through the loudspeaker, "Beeeep . . . Students, it is time for you to join us in the gymnasium for The Zones of Regulation assembly."

Vivian is so grateful for the interruption. She notices her throat relax and her breathing slow down without the attention on her anymore.

"Hello everyone, I'm Mr. Daniel. For those of you who don't know me, I'm your school counselor and I'm here to teach you about The Zones of Regulation and how we can all learn to manage our feelings. Just like we all learn about math and reading, it's also important to learn about our feelings.

Mr. Daniel goes on to say, "We can think of understanding our feelings as part of a journey along a road. Where the road leads is something that we will be learning more about in the next few months. So let's get started."

Mr. Daniel continues, "Take a moment to pay attention to your body. Feel yourself sitting on the hard surface. Are you comfortable? Now rub your hands together quickly. Do you feel heat or a tingling sensation?

These signals can come from all different places in our body, as you see here on this illustration. When we notice signals, such as temperature, breathing, pain, or muscle tightness, they can help us figure out how we are feeling.

For example, a rumble in our stomach tells us we're nervous or hungry. Or goosebumps on our skin tell us we're frightened or cold."

"Now, close your eyes and think about your day," says Mr. Daniel. "Think back to a feeling you had today. You may have felt tired, excited, worried, happy, overwhelmed, energetic, or something else. What were the signals your body gave to let you know you were feeling that way? How strong were they?

Noticing our body signals and energy levels to identify how we are feeling is the first step on the Road to Regulation."

Blue Zone

Green Zone

The **BLUE ZONE** is when we have lower energy, down feelings, and we might feel sad, sick, tired, or bored.

The **GREEN ZONE** is when we have calm energy and may feel focused, happy, okay, or ready to learn.

> If we think about it, we can categorize the way we feel into four colored Zones, called The Zones of Regulation. This gives us an easy way to think and talk about our feelings and energy. This is the next step on the Road to Regulation.

Yellow Zone

Red Zone

The **YELLOW ZONE** is when we have more energy and feelings get a little stronger. We might feel excited, silly, frustrated, or worried.

The **RED ZONE** is when our feelings and energy are so big that we may feel like we might burst, such as when we feel angry, terrified, panicked, or super excited (elated).

Mr. Daniel continues, "All the Zones are OKAY and are based on the feelings we feel! There is nothing wrong with feeling angry or sad. Waking up in the morning, you might feel tired in the Blue Zone. During a test you might feel worried in the Yellow Zone. During your favorite activity, you might feel calm in the Green Zone. You might be in the Red Zone feeling scared if your ride home from school doesn't come, or feeling overjoyed if you win a school competition."

Our Zone feelings are on the inside, but are connected to our behavior and what people see on the outside.

BEHAVIOR: Head down, eyes shut, sleeping
FEELING: Tired

BEHAVIOR: Sitting in chair, coloring, looking at paper
FEELING: Focused and happy

If our feelings or behaviors within a Zone are making us or others uncomfortable in a situation, or getting in the way of what we need or want to do, there are tools and strategies that can help us manage our Zone. We call this "regulation."

BEHAVIOR: Whispering/soft voice, fidgeting hands
FEELING: Anxious or worried

BEHAVIOR: Hands up in air, screaming
FEELING: Terrified and/or exhilarated

A STOP sign goes with the **RED ZONE** to alert us that we might need to stop and gain control of our big feelings and high energy. For example, if we are feeling angry it helps to STOP and think before we react.

On the Road to Regulation, we can use the Zones' signs to guide us in regulating, just like street signs guide drivers along a road.

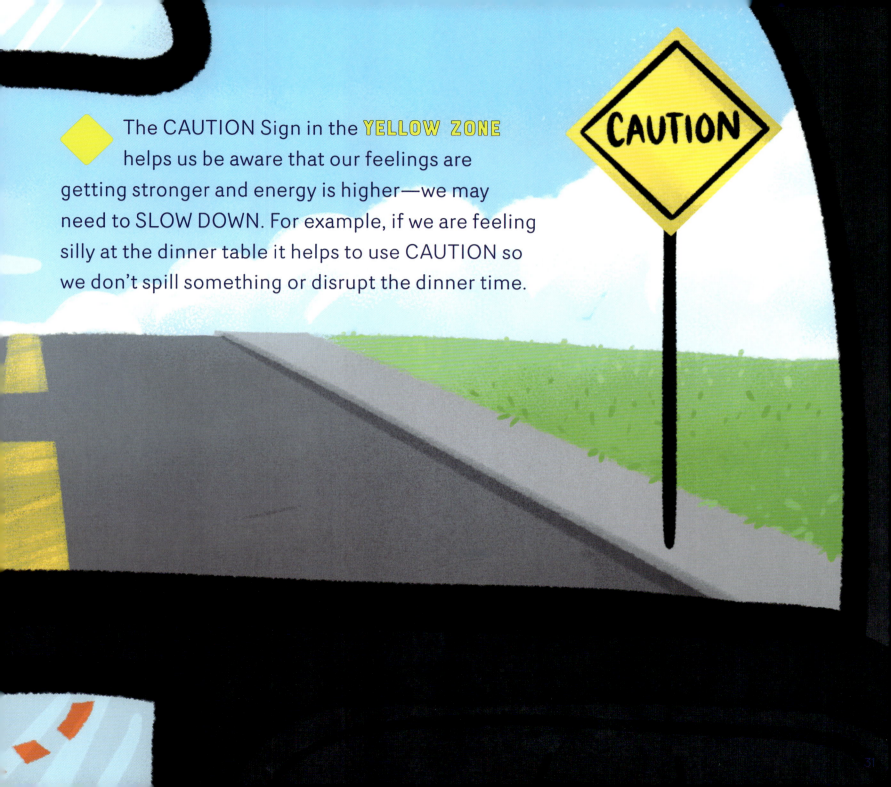

◆ The CAUTION Sign in the YELLOW ZONE helps us be aware that our feelings are getting stronger and energy is higher—we may need to SLOW DOWN. For example, if we are feeling silly at the dinner table it helps to use CAUTION so we don't spill something or disrupt the dinner time.

🟢 The GO sign is used in the **GREEN ZONE**, as we are often regulated and feeling good to GO. For example, if we are feeling focused while doing our work, we are regulating ourselves to do what we need to do.

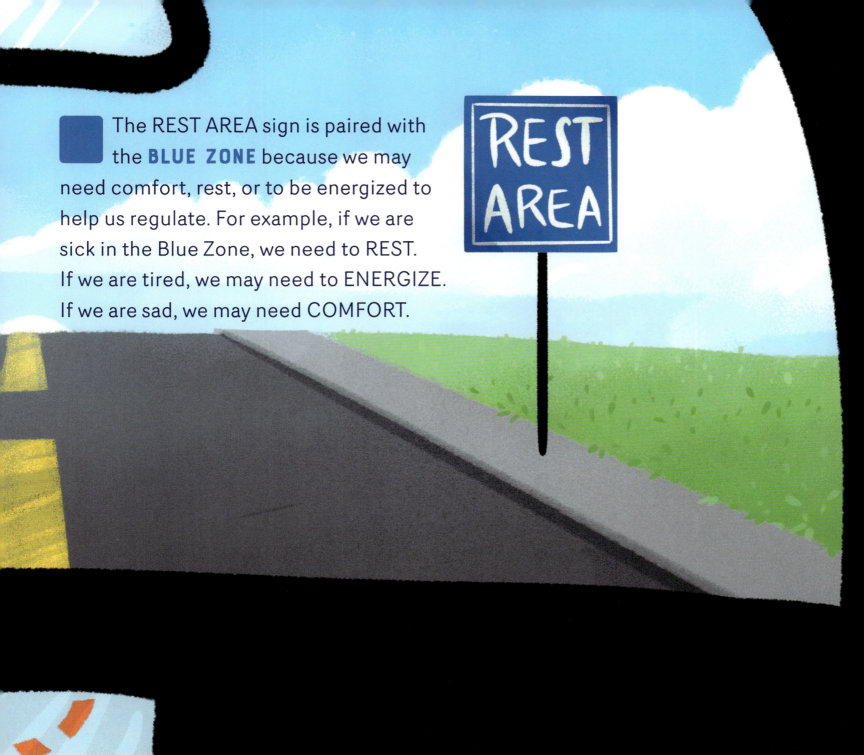

■ The REST AREA sign is paired with the **BLUE ZONE** because we may need comfort, rest, or to be energized to help us regulate. For example, if we are sick in the Blue Zone, we need to REST. If we are tired, we may need to ENERGIZE. If we are sad, we may need COMFORT.

Mr. Daniel explains, "We are all on this journey together! Here are the steps on the Road to Regulation."

"Step 1 is to see how we feel and notice our body signals and level of energy."

"Step 2 is to figure out what Zone we are in."

"In Step 3, we ask if we need to regulate ourselves. Do you need to STOP/PAUSE, use CAUTION/ SLOW DOWN, GO, or REST/ENERGIZE?"

"Later, we will teach you about tools to try on your own Road to Regulation to help you change your Zone or regulate yourself to be more comfortable and have more control within it. This takes time and is something even we adults are working on!"

At recess, Suhana races out to play kickball with her friends, feeling excited in the Yellow Zone. During the game, Suhana catches a ball and kicks the winning home run. As Suhana slides safely into home plate, she hears her classmates cheering. After everyone high fives her, she notices how quickly her Zone changed from Yellow to Red. She feels powerful and full of energy, and it feels awesome as she celebrates with her teammates.

Suhana is excited to get the win for her team, but also knows she has to be a good sport and not make the other team feel bad. She remembers Mr. Daniel saying a person often has to stop and get control when in the Red Zone. She quickly joins the rest of her team to shake hands rather than keep celebrating, which is what she wants to do!

After recess, Gabriel and Julian hurry to get in line. There is pizza and chocolate milk being served for lunch today.

Suhana walks in slowly with her head down and finds a seat. It smells so good and she notices most of her classmates are in the Green Zone, feeling happy about pizza day. However, she can't eat dairy and has her usual turkey sandwich and apple. This makes her feel left out and sad in the Blue Zone. "I guess not everyone feels the same about pizza day," Suhana thinks.

As Vivian is looking for a seat, she spots Suhana. She rushes over to congratulate her. "Wow Suhana, that was an epic kickball game, nice home run!" This makes Suhana feel proud and she forgets all about missing out on the pizza and chocolate milk.

Suhana scoots over and makes room for Vivian to join her. Talking with her friend feels comforting. She realizes she is often feeling good in the Green Zone when she spends time with her friends.

During lunch, the students hear a loud alarm go off. MAAAH MAAAH MAH!

Suhana is startled! She sits up straight and looks around with wide eyes. Julian's muscles tighten. He can't move and feels frozen with fear.

"It's the fire alarm!" Gabriel yells.

"What do we do?" Vivian asks.

The alarm is unexpected and so loud! Many of the kids are afraid. Some feel it more intensely than others.

The situation around us can have a big effect on our feelings and trigger us to move into a different Zone.

Gabriel knows it is likely only a drill, but his hands are still tightly clenched and his breath is quick and shallow. Julian feels overwhelmed with the noise and commotion.

Mr. Anthony, the lunchroom monitor, is feeling the sudden panic from the alarm going off. He scrambles to make sure everyone safely gets to where they need to go.

Ms. Lee greets her students and notices they are still a little shaken up.

"Thanks for lining up to meet me here. The building is safe. It was only a drill and we can now go back inside. That fire drill was a big surprise and I'm still in the Yellow Zone. Let's take the long way back to class to help us relax and slow down our bodies."

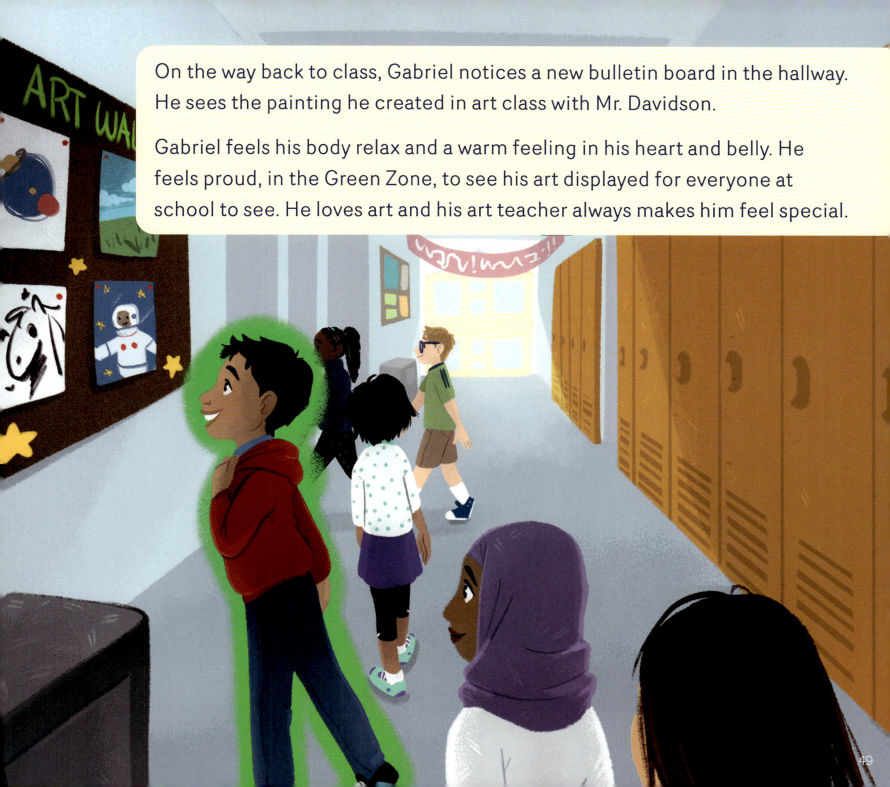

On the way back to class, Gabriel notices a new bulletin board in the hallway. He sees the painting he created in art class with Mr. Davidson.

Gabriel feels his body relax and a warm feeling in his heart and belly. He feels proud, in the Green Zone, to see his art displayed for everyone at school to see. He loves art and his art teacher always makes him feel special.

Back in the classroom, Ms. Lee talks to the students. "We can take what we learned at the assembly and use it in the classroom and at home. I put up The Zones of Regulation signs so we can check-in with our feelings and what Zone we are in throughout the day. I'll start by checking in. I'm feeling peaceful now, in the Green Zone. Anyone else want to share?"

"Well, we did have an assembly today," Gabriel offers. "Mr. Daniel taught us about The Zones of Regulation."

"What are The Zones of Regulation?" asks Nana.

"The Zones are an easy way to think and talk about feelings in my body. You know how I'm so tired in the morning and sometimes grouchy?"

"Yes," Nana replies.

"Well, that is called the Blue Zone. And the Green Zone is when I'm calm and focused. The Yellow Zone is when I get frustrated, worried, silly, or excited. And the Red Zone is when I have big feelings, like when I'm really mad or really happy."

Gabriel tells Nana more about The Zones of Regulation.

"Mr. Daniel also said that we are on the Road to Regulation all the time and we may be in each of the Zones throughout the day. On that road, the street signs can remind us about our Zones.

The blue REST AREA sign is for when our energy is down in the Blue Zone. The green GO light means we're typically *good to go* in the Green Zone.

The yellow CAUTION sign is for when our feelings and energy are getting stronger in the Yellow Zone and the red STOP sign shows us we may need to stop and get control in the Red Zone, because we have so much energy and our feelings are really big."

Gabriel goes on to explain, "Mr. Daniel told us for the next step we will learn tools that can help us regulate our feelings and energy in a Zone."

"Regulate?" Nana said, "That's a big word."

"Yep, we are going to learn more about it soon. I should tell Dad that in the morning I am in the Blue Zone, and that I am going to learn ways to help me get ready for school more easily—which I think will also help him!" Gabriel beams with pride in explaining all this to Nana.

"Sounds like a plan, darling. This seems like something we can use at home too." Nana smiles at Gabriel.

Gabriel gets a big smile too. "For now I'm in the Green Zone because it's Thursday and game night!"

EXTEND THE LEARNING: TIPS FOR FACILITATORS

❶ Read the book to introduce the characters, storyline, and The Zones of Regulation framework. (Correlates with Lesson 1 in *The Zones of Regulation* curriculum book.)

❷ Look through the story and have children make guesses about what Zone the characters are in. Find at least one character in the Blue, Green, Yellow, and Red Zone and ask children to label the character's emotion. (Correlates with Lessons 1, 2 and 7.)

❸ Identify facial expressions, body language, and situations that correspond to various emotions and feelings. Point out that our face and body provide clues to others about how people might be thinking and feeling. (Correlates with Lessons 2 and 3.)

❹ Explore the situations that unfold in the book. Ask children if they have experienced similar situations. How did they feel in the situation? What Zone were they in? Remind children that all the Zones are okay and we all find ourselves in different Zones throughout the day. (Correlates to Lesson 4.)

❺ Explore how the same situation can impact the characters' feelings and Zone differently, such as at the assembly. Discuss the different perspectives of the characters. (Correlates with Lesson 5.)

❻ Talk about how we can notice how our brain and body feels on the inside. These are sensations or signals (such as warm hands or heart pumping). Look through the story and find times when the characters experienced sensations. Ask children to name sensations they feel with an emotion, such as, "Sometimes my face is hot when I am angry." (Correlates with Lesson 6.)

❼ Look through the book and notice how a character moves through different Zones across his or her day. Ask children to talk about the Zones they have been in so far that day. (Correlates with Lesson 8.)

VOCABULARY

The Zones of Regulation: A way to think about all the different ways we feel on the inside and sort those feelings into four colored Zones. This gives us an easy way to identify, talk about, and regulate our feelings.

Blue Zone: Used to describe low levels of energy and down feelings, such as when a person feels sad, tired, sick, or bored.

Green Zone: Used to describe when we feel calm and in control. A person may be described as happy, focused, content, or ready to learn when in the Green Zone. This is the Zone where optimal learning occurs.

Yellow Zone: Used to describe when our energy is higher and feelings get a little bigger, making it a bit harder to regulate. A person may be experiencing stress, frustration, anxiety, excitement, silliness, the wiggles, or nervousness when in the Yellow Zone.

Red Zone: Used to describe extremely high energy and intense feelings. A person may be feeling elated, anger, rage, devastation, out of control, or terrified when in the Red Zone.

Feelings: The signals, emotions, and energy within our body.

Regulate: Being able to manage our feelings and behaviors in a situation in order to keep us and others comfortable while also helping us do what we need to do. This may require us to use tools/strategies to help us.

Signals/Sensations: Information from our body that helps us figure out how we feel.

Toolbox: A collection of tools and strategies that can be used to help us regulate our Zones.

Tools/Strategies: Thoughts, actions, or activities we can do to change our Zone/feeling or regulate ourselves to be more comfortable and controlled within it.

ACTIVITY SHEETS

ACTIVITY 1: COLOR IN THE ZONE

What Zone do YOU think these characters are in? Draw in the color Zone around each character to match their feeling.

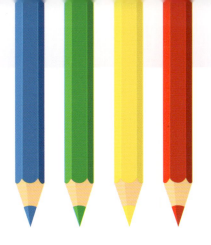

| Gabriel feels TIRED (PAGE 7) | Vivian feels WORRIED (PAGE 13) | Suhana feels DISAPPOINTED (PAGE 41) | Julian feels OVERWHELMED (PAGE 12) |
| Suhana feels OVERJOYED/ELATED (PAGE 38) | Julian feels PANICKED (PAGE 8) | Gabriel feels PROUD (PAGE 49) | Suhana feels HAPPY AND CONNECTED (PAGE 42) |

ACTIVITY 2: DRAW HOW YOU FEEL

We all feel emotions differently. Our body gives us signals to help us figure out our feelings. Below are some examples of how our characters were feeling at different times during the story. Imagine how you would feel if you were in that situation and draw a picture of this. What signals would your body give you to let you know?

Gabriel feels tired and is having a hard time waking up. Draw how you feel when you wake up in the morning.

PAGE 6

Vivian gets called on and feels nervous. Draw how you feel when you get called on in class.

PAGE 17

Julian is at the assembly feeling calm and focused. Draw how you feel when listening to something that interests you.

PAGE 26

Suhana feels scared when the fire alarm goes off. Draw how you feel when you are startled by a loud noise.

PAGE 45

Dos	Don'ts
✓ Do use this book in conjunction with the lessons in *The Zones of Regulation* curriculum for deeper teaching and extending activities and applications.	✗ Don't have the storybook be children's only exposure to The Zones of Regulation framework.
✓ Do spend time processing content from the story with children. Please use the Activity Sheets on the previous pages.	✗ Don't read through the book once and tuck it away, without following up with children on how to meaningfully apply its content to their own lives.
✓ Do create Zones visuals and use Zones Check-Ins with your children, providing lots of opportunities to check-in when they are more regulated and in the Green Zone.	✗ Don't expect children to know how to use Zones Check-Ins without practice or only provide check-in opportunities when in less regulated states.
✓ Do use Zones language to teach and support self-awareness and regulation skills.	✗ Don't misuse the Zones framework as a disciplinary technique or use language in a way that passes judgment on, or negativity toward, a child's feelings.
✓ Do model the Zones yourself, checking in and helping children see and hear from adults that all the Zones are experienced and are okay.	✗ Don't suggest or portray one Zone is worse than the others or imply the Red Zone is the bad Zone. Also don't require that only children use The Zones framework; we all work on regulation.

Dos	Don'ts
✓ Do stress that our Zone is determined by how a person is feeling on the inside.	✗ Don't classify Zones based on behavior; do not use The Zones of Regulation framework as a behavior chart where children's names are listed under Zones because a teacher or parent is happy or frustrated with a child's reactions and/or feelings.
✓ Do work at the child's pace with respect and empathy and make it accessible for him/her to check-in at all times.	✗ Don't force children to check-in or label their Zone. Don't assign only one time of day to talk about children's Zone(s).
✓ Do be aware that children with histories of trauma and/or social learning challenges may struggle with acknowledging that they are not in the Green Zone, even if it is obvious to you that they are in a different Zone. Consider mental health supports when a child doesn't feel safe acknowledging a Zone or that child continually insists he/she is in only one Zone.	✗ Don't persist in using The Zones with a child who is consistently becoming further dysregulated when encouraged to discuss the different Zones (feelings on the inside) he/she is experiencing. Consider referring this child to a counselor or other type of mental health provider available in your community.

ZONES AND OTHER RELATED PRODUCTS

Navigating The Zones

Zones Posters

New Road to Regulation poster and strategy cards for tweens and teens—Available now!

Advanced Pack: Cards to Extend Play with Navigating The Zones

Tools to Try Cards for Tweens & Teens

The Zones of Regulation integrates some core concepts from the Social Thinking® Methodology. See www.socialthinking.com to learn more about these supplemental resources.

We Thinkers! Series: Volume 1, *Social Explorers* and Volume 2, *Social Problem Solvers*

Whole Body Listening Larry at Home!, and *at School!*, 2nd Edition

You Are a Social Detective!, 2nd edition
New, Expanded, and Revised!

Superflex Curriculum

Social Thinking® and Me (two-book set)

ABOUT THE AUTHORS

Leah Kuypers, MA Ed., OTR/L, is the creator of The Zones of Regulation, a framework designed to foster self-regulation. She is the author of the book and apps by the same name, as well as co-creator of *Navigating The Zones* and the *Advanced Pack*. Leah provides trainings and consultation to districts, professionals, and caregivers on regulation and challenging behavior and conducts workshops on The Zones of Regulation framework to groups around the world. Explore her webinars and trainings on her website, www.zonesofregulation.com. She resides in Minneapolis, Minnesota, with her husband, son, daughter, and their dog.

Elizabeth Sautter, MA, CCC-SLP, specializes in social and emotional learning, is the co-owner of Communication Works, a private practice in California, and is the founder of Make Social and Emotional Learning Stick! (www.makesociallearningstick.com) where she blogs and shares resources from her books and online parenting course. Elizabeth is the author of *Make Social and Emotional Learning Stick!*, 2nd edition (2020) and is the co-author of the *Whole Body Listening Larry* books with Kristen Wilson. She presents around the country and beyond on her work and also is a trainer in The Zones of Regulation collaborative.